THE STRANGE MATTER

Ali Jane Smith

THE STRANGE MATTER

Sit Off

Are these lines as deep as they feel, or as inconsequential as they look?
Dave Marsh, *Rolling Stone*

Eclairs sweet and dainty.
What has happened?

I'll live in my old body in new ways, learning
how to be Rod Stewart in yellow satin.

The pastrymaker made the choux
stirring flour smoothly into butter

piping billowing cream into the long bubble of cooled pastry
pouring meandering chocolate along the top. What has happened?

This was a poem about the sad man selling sweet things
But he preferred to stay outside the lines.

An éclair, an éclair, an éclair, an éclair, an éclair.
One for each of the children splashing feet in the fountain.

Today, one of us accidentally did a back flip off the monkey bars
One of us wrote this poem, or at least will write it, after …

The person who leaves a chair in the middle of the room overnight
is always you yourself. It is there in the morning.

A reminder of your good intention to just sit, and think, like
a statue, a theoretical physicist, a kid with wallpaper opposite,
someone with spending money, or Rod Stewart.

Rod Stewart, coming and going
in his creamy blouse.

Remember back when I was always on the phone about
the bridge, the romantic misunderstanding, the bird
the new roof, the burial, the money problem
the mix-up, the good news, the entrance, the offer.

What has happened. This is no time for counting
on feet. I was just sitting here

thinking
did we already listen to the other side?

Aubade, Yeah Nah

I like that the morning is really just a great time to drink a series of different hot drinks each with a different kind of buzz @furiousaffects

wake to kitchen smells and stenches
reminding me of past mornings
tea routine
comforts or chafes

it's a lot
every day beginning with something
a warm drink, bread, an egg
and everything, the bowl of compost
the past, motes

I dreamt I was standing
on a sliver of
giant reed, Arundo Donax
and I was the sound
going everywhere, in waves
until I puttered out

it's weather for brown snakes
wise and frightening
it's weather for
a mildew-eating ladybug
startling spotted yellow
grazing on a powdery grey zucchini leaf
all the mildew she could wish

it's the hour for a pink and subtly-spotted
moth like a crushed gumleaf
laying eggs in leaflitter
decomposing beneath the gum tree
the hour after getting everyone
fed and dressed and out of the house
the hour for letting
the sun warm your back

there's the
reflection of my face
in the cobwebby laundry window
sunspots, scars, branching lines
there's me tipping the dregs of my tea
on earth's surface wondering
if you slice right through the ground here
is it more like mudcake, sticky
or sponge, laaaaaaaa?

rock pipes roots fungus
bacteria castings flowing water
seeping water oxygen nitrogen
slaters cicada larvae
wet turds dried turds
spiders beetles grubs dust
buried shards of dropped cups rusty iron
bones worms plastic grains of sand

let the events of the day turn liquid
as the earth can: the result of pressure.

THE CONVERSATION WITH PEST CONTROL

Not everyone knows I was once
a giant cockatoo, and the moon is an egg I laid.
I tried to keep my egg warm
but I was a drag on the tides
so I flapped back down to earth
and left her alone in the sky, cold and reflective.

Bump.
Lost my wings. Lost my beak and claws.
Soft hands, slippery mouth, plain feet.

It's been a dry, dry year. 82 mulberries
missed by the flying foxes and me
fell and were crushed, by coincidence
onto the grey pavers
in exact and tiny replicas
of Goya's *Disasters of War*.

At the bus stop a bluetongue lizard
lives beneath the warm cement.
The bluetongue always has questions
asks me to ask
the man in the street why
he is looking up into the branches of the old eucalypt?

The man points out a hive, another hive, another and two more.
He's been told to persuade the bees
out of the tree
so the chainsaw operators won't be stung.
But the queens are deep in the limbs.
The bees won't leave.

Even smoke won't make them drowsy
after a season of fire.
They're dancing the story
of the bees
on the space shuttle *Discovery*
learning to fly in zero g.

The moon has set.
The bluetongue
has warmed up and moved on.

The pest controller and me
stand earthed, contemplating
the tree I can't describe: ugly, beautiful
dangerous, safe, irresolvable, hollow
the boughs like the sturdy arms of a daughter
the boughs full of bees, keeping the tree.
A place to rest
my sulphur crest.

Things, Feelings

I walk past a woman
She says 'urgh'
I don't know if she's saying that to me
who is only trying to get past?

But I'm taking that 'urgh' with me
because starting to make nonsense
is so necessary
so flameproof
so high
so endless.

It's like being itchy.
It's like thinking you'll hurt your feet
on bindi-eyes, catheads, shattered glass.

It's like lacewing eggs on the clothesline; specks on threads.
Undrinkable water sprinkled to keep the coal cool and the dust damp.

There are seagulls lined up
seagulls wheeling
a seagull in a wading pool
standing like Lowell George's overalls.

There's plaiting her hair
like a rope
a wise serpent
the strip of brown haze
on the horizon all December, all January
like the kelp
and a seam of clay showing in cut earth.

For real?
The face of the man whose house
didn't burn down, again, last night
the bass line that gets less tentative
the chewy way of a handsewn seam.
Tired, that's a good one.
The scratch of a rake
Feel better.
The palm of his hand, a cool leaf.
Sitting down together before we go home: eat olives
talk about small fish
listen to some really high, bright sounds.
Sue the drummer and I agree
there are things
you only think briefly
the moon is something you look up to.

That's all for now.

Mary Cassatt's Hat

Tit-high horseweed a sign of villas-to-come.
No-one mows in front of branded plastic sacking
pitched to hide rubble and a muddy incline.
A chookwire fence around the corner reminds me of home.
Do not enter this property it has been sprayed with weedkiller. Do not enter.
Who's onto that outbreak of comfrey?
Forgetting again as I'm scrolling
a face, men sitting, a nice plant
a stone, up dos, coffee crema, aerial shots.
I'm here. We talked about it in Brisbane
crossing and re-crossing the river. The painter's hat
was feathered. Some of the feathers
broke away and entered
the planetary boundary layer
mixing it with gases and aerial biota.
One wants to sit on my left knee
the other one wants to sit on my left knee.
There's a lot we don't understand.
I'm staying with the horseweed panicle
imagining a future villa.

Entirely Different and Unexpected Things (said Schoenberg)

once we've walked down the hill
comparing bum notes
and seen that kookaburra
I think of going to look at blue poles
or returning to the piano in the room
an enclosed breezeway
with overexposed beams and lovely light through stained glass
it's not really a piano
I'll dry the dishes while you noodle
a fresh tea towel is just the thing, and I thought of it
I'm happy in the guide hall too
with its old portrait of the young elizabeth II
dressed like a sylphide
it must be the tulle that, for me, associates
that image with fonteyn's trembling thigh
I don't ever want to sit in a waiting room
listening to breakfast tv audio
ever ever again but some things are not a choice
why do the things that stay with you stay with you
are they caught on just two or three hooks
tiny velcro burrs in thought and experience that collect
musics, fabrics, patterns, light
a piece of buttery foil sliding around a plate
the smell of marine grease
I'm back in the stained glass room, but only in my thoughts
and the foot of the stairs
is the other place that seems to lead
to good times or the cover of pink moon or a house
on a river I saw on tv or the rooms I know only as elusive thoughts

is the fun stuff only fun if you have to do the other stuff too?
I should wake up every morning so happy
what are we doing today
we're doing this, whatever this is.

The Language of Flowers

The very glossy dark leaves of camellias
mean 'boredom'

the papery bougainvillea
means 'turning out better than expected'

and the yellow and white frangipani flowers
mean 'get it while you can'.

Some things
are strange, but not interesting.

Some biscuits
are only 'Nice', not 'Niece'.

Tonight the surf club is a dojang and people have gathered together
in their glamorous martial arts suits, sparring courteously.

Our laundry and the Parthenon
are both still standing, no thanks to the golden mean.

The dream you had that your bins moved in the night?
It's coming true. Hear the rolling wheels on the guilty footpath?

There was something before or after. Or. And.
Possum sits in the driveway.

Possum runs up a tree, but I can still see possum.
Possum doesn't act too worried.

The bird is like the tree, the bird is like the flower
the wallaby's fur is the colour of shadowed bark.

Been a predator? Prey? Know that *likeness*
means you'll go hungry

unlikeness means
you'll feel the snap of jaws.

Be a metaphor
or feel your own flesh rip.

Where's Pop? He's down the back. Oh.
Digging onion weed out of the lawn with a butter knife.

Onion weed means something's really given Pop the shits.
In the morning, back to normal.

I'm writing happy middlings.
Endings can be downers, easy ways out, or revelations

but I'd like endings
to be estuaries, full of nests.

Likes and Dislikes, Taste and Memory

Me, reading about the diaries of John Cage.
The title of this poem a quotation from his diaries.

Two women.
One puts the tips of her fingers
on her own sternum, and taps.

People make anti-poetry confessions to me. They say
"The thing about poetry is I just don't get it."
Do I say, don't worry?
Do I try and explain?
Do I say the only reason I encourage others to read poetry
is to increase my own prestige? I also wish I made more money from it.
I turn away and find
I am walking down a corridor lined with salespeople.
The one who warned me against a coconut fibre mattress
the one who said there was no real difference
between the cheapest and the second cheapest stove
the one who went out the back to get the colour I wanted
and the one who sold me   a pair of boots
too big for me.

The salespeople and I walk to the end of the corridor together.
We arrive at a stony beach.
My brother is watching a pair of sea eagles
take it in turns to fly and strike over the water.
My brother, the salespeople and I stand and watch the sea eagles
until we are sure they have caught something
and we feel we can go home.
My brother and I have talked about stones before.
He told me about the work of the anthropologist
and I told him about the collector of minerals.
For this reason, there is no need to discuss the stones on the beach.
If we see one that is notable
We hold it up.

Both Leaves and Letters

for Linda Godfrey

And when the tenantes come to paie their quarter's rent,
They bring some fowls at Midsummer, a dish of fish in Lent;
At Christmasse a capon, at Michaelmasse a goose,
And somewhat else at New-yere'a tide, for feare their lease flie loose

George Gascoigne

Fowls at Midsummer

Crispy skin chicken noodle soup—sold out.
I'll have the duck with the thick-stemmed choy sum.

Good flavour, but I miss the idea of the cleaver
in the three neat pieces of the absent chicken.

At another table a young couple
welcome a third to their party.

They look nervous and warmly intentioned.
The little white bowls, the chopsticks and spoons

crowd on their table like happy peasants
assembling to dance and sing.

A dish of fish in Lent

Lifejacket irritates my sunburn, petrol rainbows in the bilge. We find a spot.

The fish I could not hope to catch is round-eyed fish-shaped, spangling.

When I wind in my line there is a plate-sized crab. The crab and me are shocked.

At Christmas, a capon

A letter from S.T. Coleridge to his friend and fellow poet, Robert Southey (abridged):

On Xmas day I breakfasted with Davy.
I do not know what to say to you
of your dear Mother.
My Relations wish to see me.
Remember me to Mrs Lovell.
Poole asks to be remembered to you.

My bowels, my dejection of spirits.
Life, gangrened. Not domestic tranquillity.
Not a sweet wife, not a house in Whitcomb.
I wish to avoid the uneasy
feelings I shall have.
So much for me.

At Michaelmasse a goose

I have no autobiographical goose. Clearing off the fridge I find a note written to myself, just a name, 'Lin Ostrom'. Could this be something for the difficult Michaelmas section of my George Gascoigne poem? I look Lin Ostrom up again, she's not a poet at all, she's an economist who wears bright embroidered blouses and won the Nobel Prize for research into the sharing of common resources. Why did Lin Ostrom's name make me think of geese? Did I mix her up with Mary Oliver? I look instead for dictionary geese. Gander, gosling, grazing, hissing, forced, sauced, necked, bumped and stepped. A gaggle of goose words in English, but geese are scarce in the supermarket freezer. Too big, Linda says, a goose is a large bird. You need company if you intend to cook a goose.

Somewhat else

Juicy, uncoaxable purslane
in plain dirt beside the footpath.
I use my thumbnail to slice off
a stem to plant beside a stalk
of quivering variegated mint
another thumbnail cutting taken
on an early evening walk.
If they get along, they'll get along
in their terracotta plastic pot sharing
soil, water, air, light.

Thorny, Juicy

NIGHTBREATH
DAYSWEET
STONECROP
WATERSTORER

gold of sunsets
gold of heavy earrings dragging at a lobe
gold of breakfast potatoes in San Francisco
gold of BBQ chips
the gold of molten glass

things the fire makes from sand, ash
lead to other things
rearranging atoms in time and time and time
like slicing through a loaf
entropy: crumbs

solid with the molecular shape
of a liquid
toeprints after a dance on the sand
irregular, random, distorted
yeah, sounds about right

whatever's on your mind
whatever's pushed or pushing
the light moves through some things
bounces off others
every atom on a different trip

NIGHTBREATH

DAYSWEET

STONECROP

WATERSTORER

we've walked past tree trunks
shaped like femurs
creatures hide themselves
frogmouths, bats, cicadas
wait for their hour and season

now the dragonblood trees
branches like open arms
working their slow way
to the stern blue sky
drawing water from air to earth

the walk the mountain
the sky the tree
plump aloes
scarred cactus
glass slubbed

plants like fleshy thumbs, hairy tongues
grow to light/shade damp/dry earth/air
thermos morning tea spot, drowse of voices
turn the sleeping bubbas face to the shade
sit with the sun on your back

NIGHTBREATH
DAYSWEET
STONECROP
WATERSTORER

gold of tea
getting cool enough to drink
because the atoms slow
it is today
it is today

Clodhopping

Cut a hole through the ceiling, the insulating batts, tin sheets
climb out that way, spacetime jelly-wobbles.

I might revisit the demolished pub, say something else at the rock pool
decline the offer of a garden tour, take my plate out to eat with the others

give water to the thirsty bird, walk past the walk-in wardrobe
never think about the toaster oven or even the kitchenette

decline the second cup of coffee. On the sidetable a box of tissues.
A dry eye, I got lost on the way out, matt corridors

a house in a dream, a trustworthy figure directing me to exit
the warped, exuberant magazines, the yellow daisies with tawny centres

the prohibition, the fat black bear, the flat pack pear, the fact I'm here
the flattened ear, the greek key curtains red in the photograph

ice cream container full of leftover barbecued steaks.
The aluminium ladder in the aboveground pool

sinking slowly on one side. I was wearing a bouclé
v-neck jumper, mustard yellow, and I didn't feel like talking

Quarry

The 53 bus rollercoasters Robsons Road.
My small son and I sit up the front.
From every crest we share a lordly view
William Street, Cochrane Street, Shepherd Street.
The bus stops near the copse by Buckle Crescent.

I see a dark shape, furry and alive
A kangaroo? A little horse?
It's a deer, a deer, a garden-wrecking
Rusa deer, down from the escarpment
hungry, or forced out.

It strides up to the bus and climbs aboard
head tilted to manoeuvre antlers.
The driver overlooks the lack of fare
roars uphill and swings
into Mt Keira Road on amber.

My son turns to stare, and I twist too
a hand on his quickened ribs. I'd like
to touch that thick, chocolate-coloured coat.
The smell of roses on its breath exotic enough.
The deer nods, sets us at ease

with a comment on the weather.
It's been a mild, dry autumn
not much feed on the escarpment.
"We come down to your gardens at night.
Eat what we can 'til we're chased off."

'Whoso list to hunt, I know
where art an hind, I say
under my breath, but the deer
wags its antlers. "No hind I."
A sigh. "Poets have neglected us of late

yet here we are game as ever", blushing
at its pun. "Our position is awkward.
Perhaps we're best forgotten."
"There's Elizabeth Bishop's Moose", I offer.
"And Martin Harrison mentions a white-tailed deer.

One of his flashes of white in a landscape."
It's probably tactless to bring up Stafford's
over-solemn 'Travelling through the dark'.
I prefer the sad wit of Gascoigne's 'Woodsmanship'
a poem about—I don't know what—letting live?

My son breaks in with a verse of
'Rudolph the Red Nosed Reindeer'.
The Rusa laughs. "A jolly song
that holds a sort of truth.
Not the silly nose: I mean the young buck

at first excluded, going on
to lead the herd." Another sigh.
The Rusa raises its head.
Looks out at the shops and cafes.
I don't want to leave things awkward so I ask

where he'll hop off. "Just before Springhill Road. I'll graze my way across the golf course to the beach. Find out what seaweed tastes like before someone comes for me."

THE OLD LOAF

Oh yes, as soon as a new loaf of bread comes into the house
the old loaf starts to look shabby.
It becomes a chore to saw through it for toast.
A shame to pair it with silky butter when the new loaf
is boldly offering its pouter chest. That old loaf.
Rubbing up against vegemite, fig jam, rough cut marmalade.

Just a few days ago I carried the old loaf home
and laid it reverently on the bread board. I sliced
some straight away, made it into my lunch
with cheese, curly greens, something
sharp—pickle? tomato?—and ground pepper.
All too soon, the loaf's end is cut
into crumbing pieces, arranged
on racks in the hot oven
then laid out on that same bread board.
I rub each piece with a clove of raw garlic
thinking of George Orwell
and some of the things he learned about hunger.
It's time to eat onion soup, the last of my old loaf
just beginning to grow soft, sinking
under the bowl of my spoon.

Bung

mental pictures figures posed in the fringes of the bush
walking pushing a handcart on horseback waiting in the sulky
carrying milk cans grog tired children umbrellas
hauling cutting slashing digging squatting
a strange tenuous life what's all around them invisible

Stella's mother BANGS the cutlery onto the table
her EXPERIENCE edges Sybylla in gigot sleeves
her own ARMS like pikestaffs or the limbs of a spotted gum
she wants to RUN as she once wanted to SIP TEA
WILD for some solitary chaos but its WASHDAY

soapscum imitates frogspawn in the roiling water of the copper
flies flies flies flies flies flies flies flies flies flies
children red with waves of outrage eating eating calling out
a bag of broken biscuits the colour of dirty fleece or summer paddocks
pieces of whitewashed stone arranged into a town

chimney doornail war landtheft massacre kidnapping
rape beating imprisonment forced labour surveillance exile
life and land cracked like a chest
pick up threads push edges together
grieve mend gather sow

early in the day eucalypt leaves are plump crisp-edged
as jellies just turned out of their molds
the water tastes of the country we live on warm bread dripping
spread with a bone handled knife make the wrong name for another mountain
sugarloaf for the shape it makes seen from a distance

close up here's milk blood skin sky rivers
the plough turns honeycomb earth to lines
each furrow runs alongside sod already turned
scratching the surface
rips the guts out

Visions

The presenters come to me.
David Attenborough is always first.
Today he sits waggle-kneed
on the closed lid of the toilet
while I half-heartedly rub
at the ring around the bath.
It's the young David, in shorts.

I'm outdoors trying to make all of the washing
fit on the line when Griff Rhys Jones and Tony Robinson
materialise in identical red anoraks.
Tony wants me to dig. Griff thinks it doesn't matter what I do.
Monty Don avoids my attempted gardens
but his eyebrows appear like the Cheshire Cat's smile
when I'm looking for a reliable pencil.
If I see Kevin McCloud approaching in pressed denim
I turn my back and get on with rescuing lego
from the vacuum cleaner's compact brick of dust.
Brian Cox manifests as I'm getting a meal on the table.
He uses the muscles around his eyes
for emphasis when explaining
the second law of thermodynamics
but doesn't stay to eat.

On an almost empty bus, the one
I've been waiting for, Professor Mary Beard.
Waist-length grey hair, long legs
the voice of a practical neighbour.
On her blog she has written "one should only
very tentatively pontificate
about places one visits, but doesn't really understand."
How to arrive at understanding?
First press the buzzer and alight.
Mary asks, "What happened to that pencil?"

Front Yard Reverie

Air out the pop-top caravan
it's stopped raining
though rain's forecast
the sunny morning
a break in the wet week.
Everything's perfect
on this particular piece of concrete
in Gipps Street.
Air out the pop-top caravan
stand beside it
watch the sky.

Over Mt Keira
cloud assembles itself
turning the mountain moody green.
The lawn needs mowing
but I'm airing
the pop-top caravan.
Next door has a nature strip
so thick and soft you could be
walking on an inner spring.
In the caravan we sleep on
thick foam rubber that converts
into banquettes. Fold out table
with the gold pattern
reminiscent of a map
one slender silver leg
clips in to the floor.
If not perfect
then perfectible.
If not everything
then something
some world like a snowdome
for a few hours or weeks.
Is that a drop?

Bucolia

No rush today, we finished breakfast early and set out
as for a ramble, though we're taking
the commonplace walk to the bus stop again;
on one side of the street, the footpath, but today
we take the other, the grassy verge interrupted by driveways
for the novelty value and because
walking on grass brings on the pastoral fantasy
our scuffed elastic-sided boots, two large, two small, stepping carefully
across steep banks of lawn, some mown
some abandoned, at this time of year, to the heady freesias
adding to the fancy that we're walking through expanse
a field a pasture a paddock a moor a meadow a mountainside
bees amongst the flowering clover as we walk past
the house where they keep a pet pig, the house
where the man is always in his garage
the house with a freshly painted driveway, the house of the widow
the house with the lemon trees, the flats
with a pair of Dobermans on the ground floor balcony.
Eyes averted from all this
for our visit to the pretend countryside.
Elsewhere: bars, parties, offices
the theatre, stiletto heels, restaurants.
Still to come, the bus trip, a game of I Spy
played with colours instead of letters
try it, you'll notice the yellows
reds, blues, silvers, pinks and greens
and when the freesias are gone, the tree on the corner
will be covered in ripening mulberries.

Another Literary Life

after Laurie Duggan

An old new and selected on the kitchen bench
beside a bowl of prickly chokos
I can't bring myself to peel, slice, cook and eat
despite the melting welfare state and icecaps.
I'm reading an approachable analysis of the debt crisis
while the children are preoccupied with scraping
the crusted remains of breakfast from their dressing gowns.
Today's lunch is good-enough fishcakes
a celebrity chef's recipe, potato replaced with sweet potato—
a vine I've always meant to try and grow—
to lower the glycaemic index. I consider at times my life
a lucky escape from non-being. The audible traffic
shuffles between places mentioned in Blue Hills
a line, a burst of internet window-shopping, another line.

An old new and selected on the kitchen bench
despite the melting welfare state and icecaps
the crusted remains of breakfast from their dressing gowns
a vine I've always meant to try and grow
shuffles between places mentioned in Blue Hills
beside a bowl of prickly chokos
I'm reading an approachable analysis of the debt crisis
today's lunch is good-enough fishcakes
to lower the glycaemic index. I consider at times my life
a line, a burst of internet window-shopping, another line
I can't bring myself to peel, slice, cook and eat
while the children are preoccupied with scraping
a celebrity chef's recipe, potato replaced with sweet potato
a lucky escape from non-being. The audible traffic.

An old new and selected on the kitchen bench
a line, a burst of internet window-shopping, another line
beside a bowl of prickly chokos
shuffles between places mentioned in Blue Hills
I can't bring myself to peel, slice, cook and eat
a lucky escape from non-being. The audible traffic
despite the melting welfare state and icecaps
to lower the glycaemic index. I consider at times my life
I'm reading an approachable analysis of the debt crisis
a vine I've always meant to try and grow
while the children are preoccupied with scraping
a celebrity chef's recipe, potato replaced with sweet potato
the crusted remains of breakfast from their dressing gowns
today's lunch is good-enough fishcakes.

An old new and selected on the kitchen bench
while the children are preoccupied with scraping
to lower the glycaemic index. I consider at times my life
beside a bowl of prickly chokos
the crusted remains of breakfast from their dressing gowns
a lucky escape from non-being. The audible traffic
I can't bring myself to peel, slice, cook and eat
today's lunch is good-enough fishcakes
shuffles between places mentioned in Blue Hills
despite the melting welfare state and icecaps
a celebrity chef's recipe, potato replaced with sweet potato
a line, a burst of internet window-shopping, another line
I'm reading an approachable analysis of the debt crisis
a vine I've always meant to try and grow.

Ostinato

Jupiter's gravity sends meteors spinning toward us, sometimes one
One maybe hit the moon, maybe made the moon look like cheese.
Our fragile, pale moon, a dream about porcelain already falling

Oh moon, oh moon, if I loved you as I should wouldn't I keep
But I've got trivialities to get back to, don't you know, moon, about
about tv shows and knitting and making a sandwich for tomorrow?

Remember Lenny and Narelle's place in Wombarra, by now fallen
We could watch you moon, your reflection on the ocean, close, as
in a bowl, a straw mushroom floating in tom yum soup.

I'll see you in the morning, moon, walking to school, *look kids*
pert in the dayblue sky, the moon, the moon, imperfect,
sometimes impacts arrive, we're still working it out. Go round

hits Earth.

from my hand.

gazing?
the dishwasher

or knocked down.
though sitting

there's the moon
impermanent
again.

Getting Close

All the flour comes rushing out of the bag
spreads all over the counter.

What a time it takes to get somewhere a long way away.
And then I'm there. And it's a long way back.

And I realise things about where I am and where I was.
I thought I'd talk it over with the monarch butterflies, they were

I walked through Wombarra cemetery and stood at the tip of the
I asked a whale, how do you travel far, and ceaselessly.

I felt her answer through the rocks and bones, she said it's all home
the coast, the open ocean, underneath and on the surface

this is all ours and we are it, we know what to eat, what to spit,
when to dive, we sing and we listen, aren't you the same?

I'm teetering, but I get a good grip on a headstone and steady
take the slow breaths, sit down under a gum tree. I'm just going to

Because then I've got to get up and start chopping at that tree. It's
Chop, I go, chop. Chop chop coph chop coph coph chop chop

The cedar dust gets into the seams of my pockets, gets into my
I'm going to catch the train and look out the window at the

I won't see Nellie Melba, I won't see DH Lawrence, I won't see
Anna Pavlova, I won't see Mick Jagger, I won't see Lionel Rose, I

busy so

headland

to us

when to surface

myself
sit here for a minute.

not a gum, it's a red cedar.
coph.

lungs. When I've made enough from chopping
country.

Little Patty, I won't see Our Glad, I won't see
won't see C.J. Dennis, I won't see Strop

I won't see Annette Kellerman, I won't see Mark Twain, I won't Cossington-Smith, I won't see The Banjo, I won't see Arthur Boyd.

I'll see women emptying buckets and women in early labour and and little babies in their prams and sick kids at windows and old

I'll see camps near the creek and I'll see pickers who don't get paid and domestics who don't get paid anything and whose children

I'll see good girls and naughty girls I'll see brave fellows I'll see fires and lamps and stars and then just night night night through

It's starting to be morning when we get there. The night lasted a No wonder it took so long, the train has ended up in Istanbul. All

In Istanbul, bread, cucumbers, tomato, fresh cheese, little fish And after tea it's time for more tea on the ferry. The sun is going

Their talk becomes a pleasant murmur, the water is bright gold like a train, it's time to go home, but where's that again, remind me

see Johnny O'Keefe, I won't see Grace
I'll see station masters and fettlers

kids playing in big gangs
people on verandas

much
are taken away from them

bullies. When it gets dark I'll see
the window of the train.

long time, a hundred years.
I want is to splash some water on my face.

cooked over hot coals in a biscuit tin. Tea.
down, all the passengers turn to silhouettes.

and deep gold, the ferry rocks
would you, remind me, remind me.

Parts

Tippi Hedren calls up Janet Leigh.
"Janet, I love that scene where your character decides to take the
"That's so weird, Tippi," Janet replies, "because my favourite part
is where you and the schoolteacher smoke a cigarette."

"Perhaps we are the only two people who like those parts best,"
"I think your movie would have been better
if you'd used the money to start your own little motel.
I know mine would have been better if the birds all stayed normal
I would have had it tough enough working things out with Rod
and his mother—sorry Janet—and the schoolteacher, without all
But it's probably just you and me that think so."

"Well," says Janet, in a confidential tone, "I happen to know
that the woman who is writing this poem agrees with us completely.
Her favourite parts in our movies are the parts where everything is
You know, where people drive cars, pack suitcases, buy tickets
put coats on, take them off again, with perfect ease.

In fact she was just thinking that some of the most
emotionally intense moments of her life
happen when everything is sort of boring
except that she just can't bear
to put somebody's shoes on for them
when she knows that person is perfectly capable
of putting shoes on for themselves.
It's hard for her to explain why these moments
fill her with anguish, fury and despair.

forty thousand dollars."
of *The Birds*

Tippi said.

and didn't peck me.
Taylor
that pecking, you know?

ordinary.

She says imagine a wide shot of the entire kitchen, dirty dishes,
then a closeup of her children's unwashed faces and their unbrushed
a flashback to herself as a child, behaving in some awful way
then cut to her children, now adults, unable to dress themselves in
"But Janet, do you know if she ever DOES get the children to

"Well, it worked out okay this morning, Tippi
because Grace Kelly arrived at about 8 o'clock
and she made the children's lunches and put on their shoes.
She helped them brush their hair and clean their teeth.
Then they slipped into their coats and Grace walked them to

So the woman who is writing this poem
checked into a motel, and nobody stabbed her, no not even once.
She had a great time, lying in bed, reading and drinking instant
And then she checked out in time to pick up the kids
and they all went out to eat.
It was the best movie I ever saw.

END.

empty lunchboxes
teeth

time to keep appointments.
school on time?”

school.

coffee with longlife milk.

The Walk

Until I walked it every day
I thought this street was blank, brutal.
Now it is mossy with incident.
A lawn patched with purslane, windfall
oranges rolling down a driveway
the small truck that brings the bobcat
the strange matter of the plastic milk containers
suspended upside-down, the painter's scaffold
the bus stop where earlybirds pick up bumpers.
Outside the vet's an unhappy man
holding a jar walks a leashed labrador.
Demolition, construction, dog turds, it's all go.
A flaneur should have no purpose
and I have several, this is a utilitarian walk
but why not look around anyway?
Through the glass double doors of Julio's Pizza
the staff and customers appear as a tableau
around the orange laminate counter.
On days without clouds, or mist
you can raise your eyes from street level to find
Mt Kembla and wish it unaffected by the
traffic and the footsore trundlers
of shopping carts alighting
from the bus.
Wishing, too, that I had paid
more attention years ago when a visitor
explained how a refrigerator works.
You never know when these things
will be useful as a metaphor or for actual
refrigeration. Some days I have a newsreel
of bloopers from my life running in my head
inescapable replaying of my mistakes

and misunderstandings, my gaffes
and stumbles metaphoric and literal
but today I'm sanguine all the way along the street.
Every petrol station looks clean and home-y
the traffic rolls rather than hurtles
it's a good night for soaking a double
handful of navy beans in the lone
survivor from a nest of pudding basins.
I could think about plates, bowls, pretty saucers
for a long time. Susceptible, on the way to
Tony's Chickens to nostalgia for things
I didn't much care for the first time round
but I've read recently that
nostalgia is adaptive, so, let's reminisce—
a bonfire of lopped branches
and coruscating cardboard
the Catherine wheel nailed to a hardwood
fencepost, spinning and screaming.
Limestone outcrops like faked photographs
of the Loch Ness monster, humping
in contours across the hill, hawthorn
running along lost fence lines.
In old photos the bush
is striped a greenish black but I'm not sure
if the green came from
the aging print or from imagination.
The mind is a silk-satin pillowcase
folded very small. Shiny fibres rubbing
sparking, unfolding into the Goldberg Variations
Disney Princesses, fission, fusion
basketball and flight.

THE JANUARY PUZZLE

Holidaying at home, we linger over breakfast.
Sometimes the Weet-Bix packet sits on the table all day.

Breadwinning adults trickle back to work, but some of us stay with the kids
in the gradually warming waters of the public baths.

My tumble-turning days are probably behind me. My job today to drop
fifty-cent pieces into the deep end. One duck-diving kid holds up

a tiny pale seashell revealed as an acrylic fingernail.
Some Mum or Nana's manicure ruined. There are more wonders:

the saxophonist carrying a pool noodle, an ibis eating
hot chips from a bowl, a pair of aluminium crutches

discarded in the street. During the bus ride home the driver
brakes hard to avoid a deep-red camry. We are briefly jolted

one unlucky fellow-passenger slams her teeth
against the seat in front and hops off, hand over mouth.

I'd like to get home to my secondhand jigsaw. Piecing together
rambling roses in suspense, wondering if I'll find it's not all there.

Cockroachery

No evidence that
cockroaches tell time
by the large plain face
of the clock we bought

from Kmart to replace
the clock that fell
and smashed
my cobalt teacups.

At the same hour every night
they make the long journey
from the immovable dresser
to the bookshelves.

We say they 'creep', they 'scuttle'
why not say they run, as gazelles do
or a hare, in the low light
they've waited for.

Are these lonely indoor
cockroaches the same
as those living, high-density
in the compost heap?

The sound they make
in a layer of dry leaves
is something Steve Reich
might hear in a dream.

It's a long time since
I've reached for a shoe
to bring down CRUNCH!
on a running cockroach.

Not because I've reconsidered
the value of cockroach life.
I'm lazy. Or, more kindly
I accept these cockroaches

are with us. Can be reduced
but not annihilated.
They mate, lay their precious
eggs, nymphs hatch, a lifecycle

studied by pest controllers.
No evidence that cockroaches
understand the lifecycle of my species.
Unimpressed by our big brains

they require only that we drop crumbs
slough skin, use soap, paper, glue
in a warm paradise of dark corners.
Conquered, I'll call myself a natural

philosopher. Grow a beard, observe
the nocturnal sprint dispassionately
one opposable thumb on the tv remote
the worn-out couch my hide.

Northcliffe Drive, Berkeley, NSW

Northcliffe Drive extends like tickertape
but the 34 bus takes a turn into Winnima Way.
Supermarket, post office, takeaway.
Leonard Cohen never sang "I remember you well
in the Berkeley Hotel" but he might have.

Houses sit up facing the lake
like Nans in aluminium chairs, watching
the lake's edge gathering.
Someone's in up to their armpits
a wetsuit and a bucket.
Someone's riding their little sister's pushy
one-handed, back to the skatepark
with a box of Hot Food 2 Go.
A row of waiting kids dangle their legs
over the edge of the half-pipe.

Tall grass makes a meadow
draws midgey insects for the birds.
Wild fennel gives off it's good smell.
She-oaks make use of the breeze
for their whispering. Two women sit
on the same side of a picnic table
listening out.

On her drive to the Little Tern nesting site, the Ranger
gives way to the bus as two lanes become one.
The headline in that day's paper is optimistic:
"Threatened bird's future takes a tern for the better".
The first nests in forty years
each nest, "a scrape in the sand".

The chary ranger thinks up more tern puns.

DAVISTOWN

My turn with the binoculars.
The Honeyeater flies straight into the sliding-glass-door.

My brother. My yellow t-shirt. His.
My sister's curly red hair, same as mine.

My somersault into the nasturtiums.
My best friend. Wendy.

My hands squeezing margarine.
My pumpkin left on the plate.

My sniff-of-chlorine swimmers.
My not-right bike. My ugly, comforting bedspread.

My discovery under the house.
My daydream about the wallpaper in the bathroom.

My lunchbox smell. My lost cardigan.
My hot head. My idea. My vomit.

My short walk to school. My milko. My postie.
My favourite tv show. My other favourite tv show.

My voice on the tape recorder. My itchy scab.
Shops. The beach. The Chinese Restaurant. The radio.

Big Arms

There's room for an ample bum in these injection-moulded chairs
we know from barbecues and marquees, draped in white

like tipsy debutantes. Dry and comfy, we watch our playful, dogged
or scared miserable kids chug up and down with kickboards.

When you *love swimming*, what is it you love?
Water's cling, it's fascinating slop, the looming, alluring, deep end

blue and grey feeling of early, your feet and knees
not how they look, what they can do, the funny sideways

competitive friendships, lollies, the warm car that takes you home?
The acoustic of the indoor pool that lends itself to contemplation.

Let's pull my chair a little over the raggedy finish of the concrete
hardly even lifting my tired feet, a pleasure to sit after a morning

picking up pyjamas, buttering toast, brushing nightwild hair.
Resettle off-kilter and one leg of this ugly, useful, perfectly

replaceable chair drags like the battered hoof of a ruminant
content to flock among the mums and dads and grannies

their tired, enraptured faces watching unrepeatable children
outstretched arms, thrashing legs, learning to kick kick kick kick kick.

Mogul

How long since he'd sliced and salted a tomato?
There was almost nothing he touched:
silverware and bed covers, expensive notebooks
sometimes the floury crust of a gourmet burger
the younger skin of a grandchild or subordinate.

Somewhere, another old man walks through
an overgrown paddock on a morning
without frost. Waist-high in feed and weeds
the tips of his fingers touch grass and thistle
the destruction he has fostered all his life.

Synaesthesia

The ewes are run into the paddock, lambs
to the yard, castrated and docked.

After, the lambs are released, bleating.
Lambs and ewes find one another.

I thought to describe the scent
of my daughter and the best I have

is that she smells the way
the bleating lamb sounds to the ewe.

THE GALÁPAGOS

The wealth here is in variety, in detail
in the finches, iguanas, giant tortoises.

The zoologists and I walk the tortoise paths
researching the island's large and lovely testudines.

When I was small and categories were pleasure
I learned them: tortoise, turtle, terrapin;

feet or flippers, fresh or salt
like interesting beads or buttons.

Entering numbers into the cells of spreadsheets
I am reminded of the flap of gummy paper

carefully applied to hold each stamp in its album.
I'm still using tweezers and a magnifying lens

but to my pockets now I've added callipers
for measuring dung. I note insects and seeds

undigested vegetation, as Darwin
noted variation in molluscs, small

observations and measurements metamorphosed
into an explanation for our presence here.

Blessed to be privy to the tracks and habits
of the giant tortoise: heads like salted capers

mild, slow, born looking old, and longer lived
than we, their most successful predator.

I cannot write them consciousness
though the effect of their eyes is knowing

but once I watched and felt as though the
tough wrinkled skin were my own

as a tortoise pushed against the lush and supple
grass still damp, beginning the day's graze.

Bertie's Chickens and the Why

A walk through Coniston, homes and gardens arranged
around the modest soccer field
as though the suburb were an amphitheatre.
I think it must feel good to stand with a cold face
wait for the end of training, hurry home
to watch tv, eat spaghetti.

I cross Gladstone Avenue fast and graceless, no time
to mingle in the foyer and I'm glad.
I've used up my coherence by Friday night. On Friday night
I'm desperate to sit in the dark and feel something.

The theatre's full.
My seat has dusty upholstery, springs
that announce themselves to flesh
a lump of wood in the way of my right foot
but this is a good time waiting for the band to start.

Tonight the more conservative players wear
unironed shirts with Bermuda shorts and sandals.
Others feature exuberant homemade clothes.
There are pork pie hats and hats—a flat fez,
masculine pillbox—like Chris Flanagan wore in 1991.
I never saw his hat fall off, though probably it sometimes did.
They sound like The Wolverine Orchestra
colliding with Goran Bregovic.
Mel's on clarinet.
When she plays just for fun, for herself
try and be there.
A sound like finding water.

Mark is in a three-piece suit. He plays
a compressed and liberating solo
like a sparkling kitchen, cleaned in fury.
All the while, Janet's serious triceps, animated sinews
stutter beaters on a rumbling drumskin.
David (on trumpet: keeps time with his feet)
announces a piece by Bertie McMahon called
Chickens on the Ceiling.

Bertie is here, playing the double bass.
Bertie, I think to myself, I regret the time I saw you
lugging your bass
and I said "that looks heavy"
You kindly made the well-worn piccolo joke
instead of rolling your eyes.

Anyway, I was about to say.
I was thinking about gravity, the curved universe
and other things I don't properly grasp
when the blast of a trombone BLAAAAAAAAT
sticking out like a giant chook
answered my why question.
Without space, without time
no trombone blast, right?

Christmastime

Walking to yoga through
the decorated mall
snowmen big as ogres

trees, trees bauble-laden trees.
Santa's grotto is a plastic tent
but inside it's magical

Bing Crosby and David
Bowie oughta
wheel in a baby grand.

Upstairs to the yoga studio
a Chrismastimey name
for a room above a shop.

A hole in the ceiling
shows corrugated iron
and the flicker

of a whirly-whirly sucking
warm air from the roof cavity
into the sky above my little city.

Every standing asana
feels like I'm impersonating
reindeer. What would life be like

with antlers? Not
an original question.
It was asked and answered

in *I wish that I had duck feet.*
by Theodor Giesel
writing as Theo. LeSieg

who is Dr Seuss, not to be
confused with Dr Spock
who is not Mr Spock.

The boy in *I wish that I had
duck feet* soon learns its best
to just be yourself

a philosophy I've long held
though I'm still learning
the practical applications

and lately I've learned too
that self you're better-off being
is now and then an imaginary reindeer

that needn't chew reindeer moss, reindeer
moss being, not moss, but lichen
and in dwindling supply.

THE FAMOUS CONCERT PIANIST MYRA HESS

for Anna Beniuk

Borrowed goggles make a fog.
I breathe out into underwater clarity
feeling, not the survival-ecstasy of real cold
mere coolness, yet I feel so alive.
That's a metaphor, and not a metaphor.
If I said 'I feel dead' that would be metaphor only.

The goggles, the water in my ears
conjure a bubble, and me swimming inside.
You can't sing and swim
it has to stay in your head.
My frog kick is not right,
thoughts of Myra Hess distract.

The famous concert pianist Myra Hess
promised an Australian orange to the man
from the Office of Works if he would fix the ceiling
in Room 36 of the National Gallery.
The paintings already hidden underground in Wales
waited to be looked at.

"We will make no charge for the hire of the piano
merely charge for the transport of the instrument".
Most of the women in the audience
were already provided with very strong arms
from wringing, kneading, carrying potties
"bursting" into "tumultuous applause".

The Myra Hess concerts showed that ordinary people
liked that sort of thing. The ordinary audience
in ordinary overcoats, unwrapping sandwiches
listening, feeling or forgetting ordinary fear.
After the 'all clear' Myra Hess
played the slow movement again.

Without warning, Lauren Jackson enters the poem
with a backward, bum-led shuffle and leaping assertion
armpits flexed. "Lauren," I say "you are magnificent
but what are you doing here, I'm swimming
and thinking about London in 1940. This is not your poem."

"Technically, the foul's on you," she says.
"I think you want to write about Myra Hess
because in the photos she's massive, seat firmly planted on the
piano stool
big shoulders, mighty arms, she filled the room with sound.
I'm here, and I know all about what it takes to let yourself be."

Lauren's right. I want to write about
cleaning the top of someone else's fridge
mopping the floor before the visitors arrive
making phone calls with your hand pressing on your forehead
walking all over your suburb letterboxing

weighing grapefruit, wiping down tables
picking up passengers, taking measurements
entering data, changing dressings, marking papers
carrying a crying child across a car park.
Humming, with a mouth full of pins.

Bombs fell “once or twice”.
“I had to play forced crescendos to cover the noise”.
Thump thump thump thump thump.
Everything’s a mess.
Putting things together in my head
letting them out through my fingers.

Bend and Stretch

Ductility confused with tails of ducks
so A.A. Milne adorable
poking from the surface of the pond.

What are the ducks after down there?
Little fish? Elvers? The flagrant stems of waterlilies?
Something glorious in the sediment?

Perhaps the pond eels
have heard Edwardian children's literature
recited by visitors to the pond.
Sound waves travelling through water
—glob glob glob globble
glob glob glob.

At this time of day myriad winged insects hover
above the uncut grass
visible because the golden light
reflects off and shines through them.
The lawn gnats rise and fall
like champagne bubbles.
Other insects, bigger, but not much, make a purposeful flight
a beeline! Predating on the little ones.
Now a bird. Another bird.
I'd like to say they are the first
in a stuttering series of red-browed firetails
but it's a magpie pair I've started to take for granted.
Stick around, magpies, poo on the garden
I'm too squeamish and lazy
to keep chooks with their problems
of broodiness and garish foxy death.

If I'd used the time I've wasted thinking about
good and bad for entomology
I'd know more. At the museum
a woman was drawing sandhoppers.
Not insects, tiny crustaceans.
Her drawings make clear those details lost in photographs.
Later I think drawing also shows how seeing works through time
and so drawing is three dimensional in its way.
Photographs pretend a standstill.
Is that something like what Fay Dowker means about atoms and time?
Anyway, I like her voice and the way she hesitates then extrudes
boldness when its needed.

The children are designing time machines on A3 paper.
They draw in details: arrows and question marks.
Do they want to go forward, or back?
I'd like to stay here for now. Everyone
stops growing, the dust stays exactly where it is
there are no events, bread
doesn't get stale, ice doesn't melt.

Here is a photograph of Kyoto Railway Station.
I was once there, four dimensionally, but
I don't remember the shape of it. I remember walking
with my host family, I remember an enormous shopping centre
the whole thing glossy as a perfume counter.
My host sister confided, Kyoto is famous, and old.
Temples, gardens, shrines.

I saw some of these things, but I don't remember.
Now here are photographs of the famous Fushimi Inari Shrine.
More than five thousand torii gates!
Stretching into the illusion of an unending path!
That red, like the firetail's brow
not the red of blood or sunsets.

Once something's on your mind you see it everywhere.
The entrance to a block of units looks like a torii gate.
An ad in The Economist shows torii gates.
Three skinny red gum leaves on the ground make the shape of a torii gate.

A ductile person is a silly, a gullible fool.
When I was vegetarian I went to a book launch
the crowd so tight in the room
we moved according to a subtle current.
Sushi made with eel was served.
I made a mental excuse for myself, I was so
hungry, I ate. The eel tasted delicious.
I saw eels in my mind, long and mottled
swimming and brooding. I ate more and more.
I thought about eel traps, woven, a place the eel swims into
and can't turn back.

Have you any dirty washing, Mother dear?

We're the only customers at the sausage sizzle
as the retiring 747
makes its last approach

through the blue of the blue blue
blue sky over Albion Park.
At wheels down, it becomes a museum piece.

We wait in the shade of the
Lockheed Neptune we just crawled through.
Raw wood, dust and perished rubber.

Silver rivets on the fuselage like sequins on the gown
Ginger Rogers wore in Top Hat.
That dress is far away, in the Smithsonian.

The Lockheed's nosecone is a big window
made for spotting submarines.
It won't fly again

not over the startling roundabout
tucked away supermarket
green expanse for dogwalking

where three ravens collect around a scattering of jatz.
A brief and cautious flurry of beaks. Something's settled.
One eats, the others wait, uncomplaining.

We are here to look at the aeroplanes.
To see a shock of joy on the face of each person
who takes their turn sitting in the Mirage III.

The airport hangar's big enough to hold
the 747 or an exhibition of My Flaws and Failures.
The kids are bored, they've seen it all before.

The sausages need a bit longer.
People gather at the barrier.
Only moments, now, to wait.

Thoughts do what they're supposed to do
when I'm trying not to have them.
Kind of melt. It's the heat maybe

the two black coffees, the adrenalin dump
after a morning of ordinary
exhausting wrangling.

You'll need to know, the diegesis of the poem includes
Nish Manjunath's improvisation
Sue's t-shirt, this old thing!

This morning, when I lifted the soap
from its dish, it looked like
the sad diamond face of a border collie.

Stomp hop step, flap, ball change.
Your mother was right
tap is a skill for life. In the song

'Buffalo' stood for marriage, a steady job, dishcloths, all that.
Shuffle, shuffle off to buff-a
loooooo. But don't knock it til you've tried it.

As usual, it's hard to remember Bill Evans
if you're in the mood, not for love
for wandering aimlessly around the kitchen

or lying down while you decide whether or not
to do that thing you should be doing
Usually, I don't do it, then I do it.

All of this happened
but not just
as I've written it.

You can have your sausage sandwich
With onion or no
With t sauce or bbq sauce.

That's what's up to you.
We're going to eat
and watch the plane land

scrape the sides of our shoes on the tarmac
and feel these passing feelings, not wanting to go home
not wanting to stay here.

After 'Peace Piece' I like to listen to 'Some Other Time'
then stop.
Da dum.

Tom's Blues

Fairy Meadow has everything you need.
Quail's eggs and christening gowns
jazzercise and line dancing
a sushi train, a planetarium, zuccherati
special occasion chocolate cake
big enough to curl up on.
Budget accommodation, motor mowers
batteries, The Charles, antiques, activewear
naan, mist, casuarinas, rumours
superfluous bitou bush
a glitterglow building with bulky shoulders
oldish houses where rosebushes
like arthritic elbows, persevere.

Here comes a blue and white bus
with the windows flipped open.
Step up, let the door
wheeze closed behind you.

The driver turns his head.
He's wearing dark dark glasses.
Tell him where you hope to go.
He'll get you there, but you're not on his mind.
He's thinking of smoke, of light
unfocused shapes

and that line from William Blake
the road of excess
leads to the palace of wisdom.
Tom takes his foot off the brake.

Number 65 Wollongong to Port Kembla

The 65 grinds up and coasts down hills
tic-tacs the almost-too-tight bends
knits the tended gardens and green verges
of Berkeley, Lake Heights, Port Kembla
to Warrawong and Wentworth Street.

We're ahead of the timetable.
Our driver pulls over
stands on the footpath and stretches
while the extra minutes pass.

Around 10 on a fine day is the best time
to see a woman shut her galvanised gate
so a child can safely ride a plastic tractor

two people with scarves and walking sticks
struggle back from the mailbox with their mail

a thin man, tartan rug over his knees
sitting on the sunny porch
while a handsome woman cuts his silver hair

a woman in an ankle-length longyhi
who stands in her driveway
looking out toward the lake

two shoppers like quotation marks leaning close

three men who might or might not be standing together
an extended family carrying bags and a folded stroller.

It's good to get out of the house sometimes
ride the bus and stickybeak
at other people's satisfactions and frustrations.

BEWARE DANGEROUS DOG

Beware pez dispensers, oxygen tanks, wedding gowns
brushcutters, hot water bottles, wipes
highlighters, wooden spoons, old cassettes, slippery tv guides
hands, ears, wrists, watch out for lungs, tongues, skin
habits, excesses, meanness, lavished care

and if you forget where you are going
sit tight, the 65 will take you to the station.
Cross the street and catch another
back the way you came.

ASTIR WITH CARLA BLEY

Here is the sound of the bin truck
that means it's Tuesday
and too early to get up.
We used to call them 'garbos'
now comes a singular 'garbo'
who never leaves the cabin
alone whether they
want to be or not.

I'm lying here thinking about
those mornings when I put the coffee on
did a wee, washed, dressed
cleaned my teeth, put on my shoes, picked up my bag
poured that coffee into a travel cup
and walked steam-breathing
up the hill to catch the 6:37.
That's who I was and how it went.

Today, tea glass marking the cover of the book
that tops the stack, toast on a plate
beside a pile of change, a hairpin, my phone
bluetoothing to the speaker
The Charlie Haden Liberation Music Orchestra
El Quinto Regimento, in and out of sense.
This is how it is and what things are.

I meant to tell you.
The coins in that pile are worth 50 cents except
the 1966 50 cent pieces
that are eighty percent real silver.

Ann said it's the timbre that gets us
the thing you can't describe, the sound close, but not just the same
as growls, screams, cries, knocks, footsteps, heartbeats, roaring wind,
roaring water
crackling fire, bird song, insects buzzing, clicking, scraping, groaning,
aching frogs.

Here is the trumpet
an expected surprise
I drink the last mouthful of tea
the leaves are making a picture
against the morning light
that shines through
the bottom of the glass
a mushroom cloud or a broccoli floret

how will it be, today.

On and Off

Passengers!
I see you, standing
in the scant shade
of a graf-tagged real estate billboard.
I see you scan my LED display
I see your anxious signal.
                                        Come aboard!
The brief struggle with travel cards
and tickets is soon over.

Soothe your fractious child
lock the brakes on your trundle-happy walker
clasp your shopping trolley between your painful knees
swing into the convenient seat
opposite the back door.

Enjoy the ride!
Check your phone
look out the window
find a chance-met friend
peruse the Harvey Norman wishbook
fallen from a newspaper into your lap.
And when we are approaching
that shopping centre or swimming pool
school or nursery, club or office
that corner of the highway
closest to home—your destination—you may find
that it is not unique
some other hand has rung the bell
that calls me to devote the whole flank of our bus to the kerb.
Join the gentle shuffle of those who meet my eyes
in the rearview mirror
nod, or say 'thank you'
and are gone.

Words, Doing

words, I've noticed you're busy today
doing a lot of things; like warn, comfort and annoy
words
you never stop coming up with things to do and be
last weekend I'd had enough
so ready
for sounds with no words:
Ellen Kirkwood and Hilary Geddes playing
'To You, Room' aargh that's words.

I'll sleep on it words no talking
tomorrow I'll find you again
sometimes words you are
old bolts, pop rivets, drill bits
you are smashed-up reflective orange plastic
sprayed across the bike lane

ROSS HAS NEW KIDNEY
ESCHALLOTS
SCRIPS

words, sometimes you are the gum blossom
that falls for days
and covers everything
fine yellow threads
sometimes you are the barnacle scale on the fig tree
unravelled yarn
scratches on a bike frame
pile of sticks.

Storm Front, Roll Cloud

"Maybe it's a thing you could call the subgrime"
Jill Jones to Claire Albrecht

I've been looking at my hands holding the knife,
at the skins, pips, cores, stalks
at the sink filling
I've been looking at tiny writing on packets
I've been looking at daddy long legs in corners
at huntsmen stepping from crannies
the knotty hair of sleeping children
jar lids, special offers.

Angus Young plays the guitar.
It is his work, he wears a uniform.

Jodi lowers herself into the water.
"What even is everything,"
thinks Jodi.

My ordinary life feels like a dirty fleece
hard grease and soft grease
and dirt and burrs.
I'm hoping the energy to wash and rinse
that heavy, crinkled, mass
will discover me
one morning.

Angus Young
smoking a cigarette, wearing a jumper
talking to Molly
"we started as a rock n roll band
you never think you get that far
people
want you to soften it here
mellow it there."

I've been looking
                                        at the sky
clouds like Florentine wallpaper
clouds like crinkled staples
clouds like a frosty window. The sky with nothing
but a pewter-grey edge
coming in fast.
The sky cloudless. Every
        fing
                                                    thing
ting
      connected.

I've been looking at a hill of beans
and a damp coriander leaf wet and flat on the counter
feathery margins akimbo.

The knife, the wool
the sky, the burrs, the riff
the pool, the tapes, the taps.
Jodi pushes off the side
to start her backstroke
arms glittering.
Angus listens to the next question
answers with a cloud.

The Strange Matter
by Ali Jane Smith

These poems were mostly written on, and are set in, Wodi Wodi, Dharawhal and Yuin Country. My respect to the Elders, and to Wodi Wodi, Dharawhal and Yuin people. I'm not a good enough writer to describe how precious and beautiful your Country is, but I love this place.

Acknowledgement is made to the following publications in which these poems first appeared: *Australian Poetry Journal, Cordite, Cortex Journal, Demos, Famous Reporter, FourW, Hunter Anthology of Contemporary Feminist Poetry, Marrickville Pause, The Mozzie, Not Very Quiet, Plumwood Mountain, Rabbit Poetry Journal, Southerly, Tremble* (anthology of the Vice-Chancellor's Poetry Prize 2016), and the *Overland* website. 'Thorny, Juicy' was commissioned by Red Room Poetry. Some poems in this collection were funded by grants from Wollongong City Council and Culture Bank Wollongong.

First published 2025

POETRY

ISBN: 978-1-7636009-1-1

BOOK, TYPSETTING, AND LOGO DESIGN
Mountains Brown Press

PUBLISHER
Life Before Man

Gazebo Books
PO Box 375
Summer Hill
New South Wales 2130
Australia

gazebobooks.com.au/life-before-man/

2 4 6 8 10 9 7 5 3 1

This book was made possible thanks to Anthony Mark Day

COVER IMAGE: *Climb*, 2023, oil on canvas, 240 x 92 cm, © Phil Day

ISBN 978-1-7636009-1-1